Pastor Ramirez
thanks for
your help.
Jean

# Laughter in Heaven

## Finding Joy in Your Heart
## When It's Full of Tears

Barbara Jean Van Meter

AXIOM PRESS

Mobile, Alabama

*Laughter in Heaven*
by Barbara Jean Van Meter
Copyright ©2010 Barbara Jean Van Meter

ISBN  978-1-58169-357-7
For Worldwide Distribution
Printed in the U.S.A.

Axiom Press
P.O. Box 191540 • Mobile, AL 36619
800-367-8203

To my father, Cranston J. (Preach) Van Meter,
who shared his storytelling genes with me;
and to my brother, David Gary Van Meter,
whose love and support will be in my heart forever.
And to Bruce Caris who inspired me
with his childlike faith.

# Table of Contents

# Foreword

*Do not neglect to show hospitality to strangers, for by doing this some have entertained angels without knowing it* (Hebrews 13:2 NAS).

Barbara Jean Van Meter's book, *Laughter in Heaven*, brought back memories—one memory in particular. I recall how, around the age of ten, I had begun to worry about death—the death of family members, of course, but my death too. This was an inward struggle. Though I am sure my parents would have been glad to discuss this fear and reassure me, I was at that age when children are not sure they can talk about such things with others. Children worry that people will think there is something wrong with them.

But I had at that time a very powerful dream, one I later came to believe was heaven sent. In the dream I was one of a number of people who had died and were sailing in a boat across a sea towards our heavenly home. The voyage gave us time to make peace with our deaths and at the last the certainty of Jesus made every moment a wonder. When I awoke I no longer feared death and found, as a result, I had an even greater appreciation for life and its wonders.

I mention this because the memory of that dream has always helped me to sympathize with children and their fears, especially those about death. The world can be very frightening, even for Christian children. There is a basic insecurity to existence. But the popular culture often does not provide a medium for the discussion of first and last things. Sometimes you would think death doesn't exist at all. When it happens, it can seem an unnatural intrusion, even a failure on the part of the survivors. Or perhaps death has to be very dramatic, either tragic or heroic—but it is never simply a *normal* occurrence.

Death for our ancestors in the faith brought just as much sadness—but it was also normal. There was no escaping it. And Van Meter's book treats the death of a grandfather as a sad event—but also one that is as perfectly normal as, well, going out fishing with a grandson. While portraying the doubts and questions a child raised in the church might have regarding the death of a beloved grandfather, she also makes it clear that despite the child's misconceptions, the adults really care. They are understanding and more than ready to talk about the experience. Her book also makes it clear that death does not mean the end of the love we share, nor the concern we feel for each other, regardless of which side of the grave we stand on.

I appreciate that this story demonstrates heaven's concern for our weakness and recognizes that the border between the earthly and the divine is a little more permeable than some imagine. I think that some will see a resemblance here, at least a little, between the present book and *The Shack*.

Death is a reality that none of us, at any age, can escape but fortunately so is love. God's love. Our love. A child's love. A grandparent's love. For as it says in Scripture,

*Set me as a seal upon your heart, As a seal upon your arm; for love is as strong as death, jealousy as cruel as the grave* (Song of Songs 8:6 NKJV).

—*Frank Ramirez, Pastor, Everett Church of the Brethren, and author of more than thirty books.*

# Acknowledgments

Thanks to my agent, Keith Carroll, and to my editor, Kathy Banashak, for their guidance and insights as I tread into unknown territory. Also thanks to Robert M. Van Meter and Jorinde van den Berg for their "extra pair of eyes" and for their encouragement.

FEAR NOT

# Chapter 1

# The Funeral

"What's that smell?" Josh grumbled and rubbed his nose as they walked through the door of the church.

"It's just the smell of flowers," Mom said sharply. She was on the verge of tears and wasn't in the mood to deal with his grousing. Dad had already explained everything to him at home and had told him how he was supposed to act, but Josh didn't want to be there; he thought the whole thing was stupid.

*Why do you have to go look at dead people anyway?* Josh folded his arms and dragged his feet across the carpet. Josh's grumbling was on the outside; inside he was afraid of what dead

1

people looked like. All he had seen had been those scary scenes in the movies where the dead people came up out of the grave.

The low murmur of people grew louder as he followed his parents around the corner and into the sanctuary of the church. He had never been to a funeral before and wasn't sure what to expect, so he kept frowning to hide his fear.

A few people were sitting in the pews, but most were standing at the front of the sanctuary. Josh smelled Aunt Mary's perfume before he saw her; her eyes were red and she carried a tissue in her hand. Somehow she still managed to pinch his cheek and exclaim what a fine young man he was becoming.

Uncle Tim squeezed Josh's hand and pounded him on the shoulder with his other heavy, construction-worker hand. Josh forced a smile and nodded. Really, he just wanted to get away from everyone.

Josh waited until his parents began talking with his aunt and uncle; then he disappeared into the pews. Josh's eyes strained to see through the crowd, yet he looked away when he had the chance. Once, he caught a glimpse of the coffin; it was larger than he had expected.

*I guess I never really thought about how big it might be,* Josh thought. It was silver colored with soft cushions hanging over the sides. He guessed Grandpa was inside the coffin, and he wanted no part of that.

Josh began to wander around the pews, trying to avoid any other cheek pinches or heavy pats on the shoulder—and the coffin. He touched his pocket to be sure the picture was still there. The thoughts he had been trying to avoid kept returning. *What is it like to be dead? What does Grandpa look like? What will he feel like? Will his eyes be open or closed?*

Josh looked around at the people. He saw his girl cousins sitting in a group in one pew and decided to avoid them too. Instead, he examined the flowers. The yellow petals were softer than the red ones. The purple petals were long; the pistil and stamen could easily be seen. Grandpa had told him all about the parts of flowers.

He read the cards that were in the flower vases. A part of him wanted to slip back out of the sanctuary, but another part was curious.

Dad appeared, put his arm around Josh's shoulders, and walked him over to the casket where Grandpa lay. The moment Josh had been dreading had arrived.

Josh stood staring at his feet and slowly lifted his eyes to see into the coffin. Grandpa lay on the soft cushions surrounded by flowers. Josh looked at Grandpa's face. Behind Grandpa's glasses, his eyes were closed; he looked comfortable, as if he had fallen asleep on his bed with his glasses on. His face had been shaved, but the skin was too pink. *Did someone put makeup on him?* In the air was a faint hint of shampoo that had been used to wash his white hair—what little was left of it.

Grandpa was wearing a new navy blue suit with a red tie. Dad patted Grandpa's hands and sniffled. Josh kept looking at Grandpa. He kind of expected Grandpa to open his eyes and laugh as if he were playing a joke.

Josh touched the soft cushion and reached in to tap Grandpa on the shoulder. He really wanted Grandpa to wake up and for everything to be like it was last summer. Instead, Grandpa felt firm—firmer than Josh had remembered. Josh ran his hand down over Grandpa's arm to his hands that were folded one on top of the other. They were cold and hard. Josh's hand flinched; Grandpa had never felt like this before.

"Josh," said Dad, looking him in the eyes, "the outside part of your grandfather is here. The inside part is in heaven with the angels. Remember the time in school when you made papier-mâché planets? You blew up balloons and covered them with strips of paper. When the paper dried, you popped the balloons to let the air out, but the paper stayed just as it was. You couldn't see the air when it was in the balloons nor when it was let it out, but you knew it was gone. Your grandfather is something like that."

Dad looked back at Grandpa and continued, "Inside Grandpa was a part that laughed, made his eyes sparkle, and loved his family. That is the part that is in heaven. The outside part that we can see did not go to heaven."

Josh knew then that it was all true. His grandpa was dead and was not coming back. The tears that Josh had been pushing way down inside now welled up and gushed forth. He couldn't stop them.

"I don't want Grandpa to go. I want him to come back," Josh sobbed.

Dad pulled him close. "I know; I know."

Josh and his father stood there awhile then moved to the pews, and Mom gave Josh a few tissues. The service was about to begin.

Josh sat in the pew beside his father trying to squelch the sniffles and the hiccups. His eyes watched the sun stream through the stained glass windows and cast a rainbow of colors on the wall. A window near Josh showed an angel with his arms outstretched. Under the picture, Josh read the words: "Fear not."

*But I am afraid. I'm afraid of what will happen to me. Who will play with me? Who will take me fishing?* More questions went through Josh's mind. *What does it mean to die? Does it hurt? Do you die all alone or is someone with you? What about my grandfather; is he in heaven now or will he go there later?* Josh's questions just kept growing like the lump of sadness that filled his chest and kept the tears flowing.

As the people were singing and the pastor was talking, Josh's thoughts drifted to last summer when he had stayed at Grandpa's house, and they had talked about heaven.

# CHAPTER 2

## Last Summer

"Grandpa, when dogs die, do they go to heaven?" Josh asked as he baited his hook. Grandpa had taught him a secret way to wrap the worm around the hook so the tail of the worm could still wriggle freely.

"Oh," Grandpa said as he watched Josh cast upstream, "Let's see now. Is there a dog heaven?" Grandpa rubbed his chin with his left hand as he held the fishing rod in his right. "I'm not sure; but yes, I think so. Why do you ask?"

Josh looked over at Jasper, his twelve-pound black and white terrier/poodle, who was lying with her head on her crossed paws.

He whispered, "My friend, Bruce, well . . . his dog died. What's heaven for people like?"

"I've often wondered about that myself. It's a wonderful place I hear. I haven't been there yet, so I don't know for sure . . . I think of heaven as a place where everyone and everything is full of joy and love. It's a place with no pains or sorrows because God and Jesus are there. I just imagine a beautiful, peaceful place for the next step in our lives. In some ways, I'm looking forward to going there. Then I'll get to see your grandma and my two brothers who have already passed away." Grandpa gazed out over the water.

Josh sat quietly, thinking about what Grandpa had said. He felt a tug on his line, and he started wrestling with it. His pole bent as he tugged and tugged.

Out popped a tree limb from beneath the water.

"I've heard of stickleback fish but not stick fish." Grandpa chuckled.

Josh loosened the stick from his pole and

threw it across the grass and up the creek bank. Jasper barked and chased after it.

Josh lay back, anchored the pole between his legs, and watched the shapes of the clouds as they changed from rabbits to sheep to buffalo. "Grandpa, if you were in heaven, could you walk on the clouds?"

Grandpa looked up at the clouds, took out his handkerchief, lifted up his hat, and wiped his forehead. "No, Josh, can you walk on fog? Fog is just clouds that have come down from above to the ground."

"Angels can walk on them, though," Josh answered.

"Probably," Grandpa agreed as he settled his hat on his head and put his handkerchief back in his hip pocket.

Josh's rod jerked hard, and he sprang up. Jasper jumped and stared at the river as she let out a low growl. A big striped bass was swimming away, but Josh held the pole tightly and began to reel in the fish.

"That's it, Sonny, go steady. It looks like a

big one," Grandpa directed.

When the striped bass was close, Grandpa leaned into the water and scooped the fish into the net.

"Ah, ha!" Grandpa yelled. "It must be at least eighteen inches long."

"That's a big one, huh, Grandpa?" Josh asked, giggling.

"Yeah, very big!" Grandpa said with excitement. Jasper ran around barking. "We'll have to take a picture of this one!"

After dinner, Grandpa and Josh sat together on a swing on the back screened-in porch. Jasper walked around in circles until she curled up on her favorite rug. Fireflies dotted the darkness, crickets chirped, bullfrogs bellowed, and insects buzzed and fluttered their wings as they tried to reach the porch light.

"Grandpa, how do crickets make that noise?" Josh said as he stared into the backyard and listened intently to the night sounds.

"Some people say they rub their hind legs

together, but I've read in my science maga-zines that really it's only the male who makes that chirping noise to attract the female. His left wing has ribs or line bumps. He makes the noise by scraping his right wing over the ribs," Grandpa answered.

"Wow! That's cool," Josh said as the fire-flies began to light up the backyard. "Do lightning bugs have batteries to make them light up?"

"No, they have an enzyme, *luciferase*, I be-lieve it's called, that causes them to glow. Isn't it wonderful how God made the whole world—even the smallest insects—with the ability to do amazing things."

After a moment, Josh said, "Grandpa, I've been thinking. I think heaven is just like your house. All those things you said earlier—peace, joy, and love—are all right here."

"I agree, Josh, I agree."

JOSH'S MIND CAME BACK TO THE CHURCH WHEN HE FELT A TAP ON

HIS SHOULDER. He realized everyone was standing; Josh's mom asked if he wanted to see Grandpa one more time. Josh nodded his head and walked with his head down; he didn't want anyone to see the tears beginning to slide down his cheeks again. As he walked by the casket, he leaned in to touch Grandpa one last time. From his pocket, he took the picture of himself holding up the big fish he had caught last summer, tucked it into Grandpa's hand, and whispered, "Good-bye, Grandpa."

# CHAPTER 3

# The Prayer

A few weeks after the funeral, life was so different for Josh. Without his grandpa, he didn't know what to do. He walked with his head down and his shoulders slumped. He didn't even talk much to Jasper. He tried to do his homework, but he couldn't help thinking about Grandpa and missing him. The sadness still filled his chest, and tears came easily. When the kids at school saw his tears, they made fun of him.

Mom and Dad weren't as cheerful either, but they went back to work. One day Dad even took Josh fishing. They went back to the creek across the street from Grandpa's house.

Both Josh and his dad were silent as they went through the motions of baiting the hooks and getting ready to throw in their lines. Josh looked at Dad and raised his left eyebrow.

*How did Dad know the secret way to wrap the worm around the hook?* Dad caught a striped bass, and Josh helped to scoop it up with the net. Mom baked it that night with lemon juice and a few secret spices. The fish tasted good—almost as good as at Grandpa's house.

The days dragged on and no matter how hard Josh tried, the sadness still sat heavily on his chest. One day after school, Josh peeked around the front door of his home as he opened it. The coast was clear. He could hear his mother talking on the phone—probably to his teacher. He was in big trouble. His mom would never understand.

Once in his room, he emptied his backpack of school papers and threw in his pajamas, some clothes, his bear (yeah, he was nine years old, but he needed that bear now), and his favorite Encyclopedia Brown books—the one about the penguins and another book with the story about the silent dog whistle. Jasper watched and tilted her head. Josh patted her head and said, "Bye."

Out on the street, Josh began to walk in no particular direction. He just knew he had to get away. The sky was a typical dark, gray, fall day. It seemed to mirror his sad mood. He trudged along not sure where he was going; he just kept moving. As he walked the streets of Baltimore, raindrops began to fall. Even the air seemed to wrap an eerie sadness around Josh.

Josh's thoughts wandered back to how he had gotten into this mess . . .

Soon after school had started, Grandpa had gone into the hospital. When Grandpa came home from the hospital, he was different. His pale face had more wrinkles, and he had to rest most of the time.

"When will Grandpa be like he was before?" Josh had asked his mother.

"I don't know, honey. He is very ill, and he'll never be completely well again. Keep praying for him."

The next Sunday, Josh was sitting in church, and his grandpa still was not any better. He heard the pastor say that if you needed prayer for anyone you could go to the side of the altar after taking communion and someone would pray for you. Josh always walked up to the altar to be blessed by the pastor. He knelt on the soft cushion, bowed his head, and waited while the pastor cupped his hand on Josh's head and asked God to help Josh grow in wisdom and strength.

Josh rose and walked to the small kneeling bench where a lady stood waiting to pray for people. He knelt down, and the lady asked him what he wanted her to pray about. After Josh explained about his grandpa, she covered his head with her hands and prayed. The warmth from her hands spread through Josh's body as she asked for God's healing touch upon Grandpa and for God to comfort Josh.

Then she made the mark of the cross with oil on his forehead. He just *knew* Grandpa would be fine now.

A few days later, Josh was outside riding his bike when he saw his mother's car turn the corner. He knew his mom and dad had been to the hospital to see his grandpa, so he pedaled as fast as he could and rushed into the house.

"How's Grandpa today?" Josh yelled as he ran through the door with Jasper trailing close at his heels.

No one told him to close the door; no one scolded him for yelling in the house. Even Jasper sensed something was wrong. She put her tail between her legs and curled up in the corner.

Josh's dad ran his fingers through Josh's hair. It was matted to his head from the baseball cap and the sweat.

"Isn't Grandpa any better? I prayed for him!"

"Josh, son, I want you to listen carefully,"

his father began. "Remember, in church, you learned about heaven?"

Josh nodded, but his eyes were wide.

"Well, your grandfather is now in heaven. He died." Josh's father's eyes were full of tears. Josh saw his mother from the corner of his eye and watched a tear come out of her left eye and run straight down her face. She wiped it away and dabbed a tissue at her nose.

Josh stood still; he couldn't stop the tears that welled up in his own eyes and gushed down his cheeks. He couldn't swallow the lump in his throat. "It can't be. It can't be. I prayed for him!" Josh yelled as he ran to his room and slammed the door.

# CHAPTER 4

# The Old Man

BACK ON THE STREETS, Josh wondered, *What is the use of praying? If God didn't make Grandpa any better, why pray?*

When Josh heard the scream of a police car's siren, he dashed into the bushes that outlined the side of a house. *Would his mom send the police after him?* He remained hidden until the loud noise from the siren had faded into the distance.

As he crawled out from under the boxwoods, the water gushed down off the leaves and soaked his jacket. The smell of the rain-soaked leaves reminded Josh of death—everything seemed like it was dying. He felt the thump, thump of his heart and the knocking of his knees. As he wiped away the tears, he felt his right eye was puffy and tender. His knuckles were cut and bruised. He wished he had a silent whistle that only Jasper could hear. He needed Jasper with him now.

Josh took a deep breath and looked around. He knew he had to stay away from the police, so he raced across the backyard, climbed over a fence, and kept walking close to the buildings to stay dry. He walked with his head down, lost in his thoughts.

*Is Grandpa out there in the ground where it is cold and wet? Will this sadness in my chest ever go away?* Josh felt so alone. He had believed what he had been told in Sunday school and church. He thought all he had to do was pray, and God would answer his prayers. Now he didn't know what to believe.

The rain was ending. Josh looked up at the street signs, but he didn't know where he was.

"Hey, kid. Come here!" yelled a tall guy with stringy blonde hair whose muscles were straining against the black leather sleeves of his jacket.

Josh stopped. His mouth opened, and his heart thumped in his ears again.

"I said, com'ere!" the guy repeated in a deeper tone of voice. Two other guys and three girls stood around snickering. This was just like what had happened at school. Only this guy was much bigger. Josh took one step forward, then spun around and ran as fast as he could in the opposite direction.

"Look at the chick'n run," one of them called after him. Their giggling and taunting faded as Josh ran through a puddle and splashed water up the legs of his pants. He rounded a corner and flapped his arms to keep from falling when he stopped abruptly.

Right in front of him stood a police officer. The officer was talking and gesturing as if he were giving directions to a man, so Josh slinked past, lowering his head.

Josh walked and walked. He didn't recognize anything. He was getting tired and hungry; he sat on the concrete stoop of a tall, brick row house. He sat with his head in his hands and said to Jesus, "I don't know what to do." Soon more tears rolled down his cheeks, and he wiped his eyes with the heels of his hands.

"Excuse me, Sonny," a white-haired man carrying a fishing pole said as he tried to come down the steps.

Josh looked in the old man's dark-brown eyes behind his glasses. Their sparkle held Josh's gaze for a moment. They were just like Grandpa's eyes. And the smile. The smile spread across his face just like Grandpa's had done. Josh stood and moved off the steps.

"Do you live around here, Sonny?"

"I live on Parkview Drive," Josh said. It wasn't really a lie. He stayed with his grandpa many times.

"Oh, I'm headed that way now to do some fishing. The fish really bite after it rains."

*Great*, Josh thought. *I can follow this old man to Grandpa's house.* Josh watched as the man plodded off; he followed, but not too closely. They crossed a few streets and took a couple of turns. Finally, Josh recognized the street—the same street where Grandpa lived. The old man crossed the street and headed down the creek bank, and Josh followed. The way the old man walked, the way he carried his pole, and the hat—so many things reminded Josh of his grandpa. Josh had been to this creek so many times with Grandpa. He felt comfortable there—and with the old man.

Josh laid his backpack down on the ground and sat on the bank of the creek—not too close to the old man, but near enough. He watched the setting sun peeking from behind the passing clouds that had brought the rain. Yellow streaks like open fingers stretched far across the sky from the west to the east. Birds were flying and gathering in groups; they were preparing to make their migration to the south for the winter. The breeze was cool. Two trees on the opposite bank of the creek cast long shadows across the creek and up to where Josh sat. A big tree yawned and stretched its branches like arms out over the creek bank. The water in the middle of the creek trickled downstream, but the water that nestled in the roots of the tree was calm.

The old gentleman stood in the same spot where Josh and his grandfather had fished last summer. The way the gentleman cast his line reminded Josh of his grandfather too. The hook and the sinker made ripples in the water that spread into wide circles.

"Mister, do you fish here often? I've never seen you before."

"Oh, yes, Sonny. I've seen you and your grandpa here many times."

"You know my grandpa? Uh ... knew him?"

"Oh, my, yes. We've been friends for a long time."

"I guess you know, then, that we used to fish in this very spot. I caught a big fish here last summer."

"Oh, yes, I remember that."

Josh wondered how this man knew about his big fish. He figured this man must be one of Grandpa's friends and Grandpa had probably told him, maybe even had shown him the picture.

"I really miss him. Why did he have to die? Why does anyone have to die?"

The old man was bent over getting his worms out of his tackle box. He mumbled something and Josh continued. "I don't believe in God any more, either. I prayed to God to heal my grandfather, and you know what he did? He let Grandpa die anyway. What good is God if he doesn't heal people and lets them die instead? I thought God only did good things. Is letting people die a good thing?"

"Oh, my. What a question!" The old man took off his glasses and wiped them with his handkerchief.

Josh continued watching the water flow by, and the words kept pouring out of his mouth. "Ever since Grandpa died, I've had this sadness that stays with me every day. It feels so heavy and I don't know what to do with it or how to get rid of it. I don't want to eat, and I don't want to go to school—oh, school! Boy, am I in trouble."

The old man put his glasses back on and looked over the top of them at Josh.

"I got into a fight at school today. It really wasn't my fault."

The old man tucked his handkerchief in his hip pocket, picked up his fishing pole, and looked back out across the creek. "Mmm."

Josh watched the old man as he stood there holding his pole.

Josh thought, *Since he knew Grandpa, he'll probably know all about it.* Josh asked, "If you're a boy and you cry, does that make you a sissy?"

"Well, that depends . . ." the old man said, still looking at the water.

"I was sitting in the school cafeteria today looking at my fish sticks. I couldn't eat them because I got a lump in my throat. The fish sticks reminded me of the stick and the fish I caught last summer when I was with Grandpa, and I started crying. Everyone at the table started laughing and calling me a sissy. And that's another thing, why does God let people make fun of you? It hurts!

"Later outside on the playground, a group of boys who had been sitting at the table had told some other boys about me crying, and they all gathered around me and called me names. One of them, Mike, said I was a crybaby! I had enough. I just started swinging. I jumped on Mike and started pounding him. We fell to the ground. But he was bigger, so he was on top punching me." As he remembered all that had happened that day, Josh wiped his eyes with his shirtsleeve.

"At one point, I was able to roll him over and get on top so I gave him some good punches too. He flipped me over and started punching again. Look at the cuts on my knuckles, and my eye hurts! The playground monitor grabbed both of us and took us to the principal's office. I'm in big trouble. The other kids just don't understand. I'm not a sissy or a crybaby. I just have a huge, sad feeling and something keeps getting into my throat that makes me cry." Josh's tears began to fall again.

# CHAPTER 5

# Heaven

The old man anchored his pole between two rocks, sat down on the creek bank, and wrapped his arms around Josh. He took his finger and wiped away Josh's tears. "Do you really think Jesus wants you to hurt so much?"

Josh leaned his head into the chest of the old man, who patted Josh's head and rocked back and forth as more tears flowed.

When the tears finally subsided, Josh moved away and looked into the eyes of the old man. *Who was this man? How did he know so much about Jesus?*

Josh said, "But why does God let people die? Why doesn't he heal everyone?"

"Many people think prayer is telling God to do what they think is best. Humans want everything their way—not God's way. But God always knows what is best. You're looking at death as though it were something bad. But think about the caterpillar—a creepy, crawly worm that can only travel on the ground. Then what happens? It wraps itself in a cocoon and dies to its old life only to emerge several days later in a new life as a beautiful butterfly. As a butterfly, it can freely fly anywhere and live an entirely different life."

Josh sat with his head bowed, looking at his hands.

"Josh, where do you think your grandpa is now?" the old man asked.

"I guess in heaven," Josh said as he hiccupped and looked up into the sky.

*How did he know my name? I guess Grandpa told him.* He twisted his head to the left to look at the old man.

"Mister, you know my name; what's yours?"

"My name is Gabriel. Some people call me Gabe."

"That's a name in the Bible," Josh said.

"Yes, that's the name of an angel in the Bible," the old man said. "And angels know what heaven is like. Tell me, what do you think heaven is like?"

"I asked Grandpa that once, and he said he thought it was a wonderful place." Josh sniffled and wiped his sleeve across his face again.

"Well, now your grandpa knows what heaven is like. Do you think God or Jesus would have you live this life only to send you to a terrible place afterwards?"

"No, I guess not."

"Then tell me what you think heaven is like."

Josh looked around. "Well, I guess it would be a lot like this place right here by the creek. It will be a place where you will feel good— just like that day last summer when Grandpa and I were fishing, and I caught the big fish."

"Why was that so nice?"

"I don't know; it was just fun!" Josh looked down into his hands again. "Grandpa and I were together. We were having fun just fishing. It was good to be near him, to ask him questions, to know that he would take care of me." Josh looked up into Gabe's face. "Grandpa made jokes, and we laughed all the time."

Gabe smiled and looked up into the sky, "Do you think your grandpa is happy in heaven now?"

"I guess so . . ." Josh looked up at the sky, then down at his hands. "You know what? I didn't tell anyone, but I put the picture of me and the big fish in the coffin with Grandpa. Do you think he took it with him to heaven? Would that make him happy?"

"I think your grandpa and Jesus are looking at that picture and laughing—just like on the day when you and your grandpa were having so much fun. And that laughter is pleasing to God's ears," Gabe said with a smile.

Josh pictured that in his mind, and his lips began to curve upward. For the first time in weeks, Josh could smile, and he felt a little bit of the sadness disappear.

"Will all the sadness ever go away?"

The old man sat there rubbing his chin and reminded Josh of Grandpa once more. "You've been hurt, and it takes time to heal."

"Yeah, I have cuts and bruises on my knuckles, and my eye is swollen."

Gabe turned toward Josh and pointed to Josh's heart. "And you have bruises inside too. When someone you love dies, the sadness causes a bruise on the inside."

"Does that bruise make me cry too?"

"Well, sort of. Just like your black eye is tender and hurts when someone touches it, when you think of your grandpa, you are touching a part of you inside that is still tender, and it hurts. It will get better with time just like your outside bruises will get better."

"So I'm not a crybaby; I'm just hurt on the inside?"

"That's one way to put it. When you get

better on the inside, then you won't cry as easily, but you will always miss your grandpa."

"Dad said the inside part is the part that goes to heaven. Is that true? Is that why Grandpa felt so cold at the funeral?"

Gabe scooted around to get into a more comfortable position. "That's a good question, and your father is pretty smart. Yes, the part of us that loves others, cares for others, and wants the best for everyone is the part that goes to heaven. Some people call it your soul."

"Hmmm . . ." Josh looked deeply into his hands. "That part sounds like Jesus. He loves us, cares for us, and wants what is best for all."

"Yes, and that part is the part of us that Jesus wants to become more like him."

Josh took a deep breath. This was a lot to understand.

# CHAPTER 6

# Death

The sun was slowly setting. Orange and red colors were streaming out from behind the clouds. It didn't seem like the fish were biting, so the old man stood up, reeled in his line, and set it beside his tackle box.

The bullfrogs began bellowing. It was just like the night Josh had spent with Grandpa last summer. Josh felt warm with the memory; he wrapped his arms around his legs. He still had many questions about death; he also had some fears.

"Mr. Gabe, does it hurt to die?"

Gabe took a deep breath and sat down beside Josh again. "That all depends on how you die. Some people have an illness or an accident that may cause pain, but some people just die in their sleep. The pain comes from the accident or the illness, but dying is that inside part of you going to another place to live. It's a place where all the people you loved on earth who have already died are living with Jesus, and God is waiting for you.

"You know what? It's just like your going into middle school. You'll leave one school and move on to another school where all your friends are. That doesn't hurt, does it?"

Josh thought about it and shook his head. "Grandpa said he wanted to go to heaven to see his brothers and Grandma. Will I see Grandpa when I go to heaven?"

"Oh, yes. You'll see all the people you've loved there. It's a glorious place."

*How did this Gabriel know so much about heaven? This old man seemed to know everything.*

"Are you hungry?" Gabe asked the boy.

Seeing Josh's quick nod, Gabe opened his tackle box and took out a sandwich, an apple, and some water, giving them to Josh.

*How did he get so much in his tackle box?* Josh wondered.

Josh thanked Gabe and ate the sandwich. The bread was different; Josh opened the sandwich and looked at the bread. Whatever it was, it was good. Josh sat chewing his food and watching the sun set below the horizon, sending out pink and purple colors. It was getting darker. "I'm afraid to go to sleep now. Will I die when I go to sleep?"

"Oh, Josh. There is no need to be afraid of going to sleep. Sleep is good for you. People who die in their sleep usually have been very sick. You know Jesus said that he would neither leave you nor forsake you. That means that any time of day, or even in the middle of the night, you don't need to be afraid. Jesus is watching over you."

That made Josh feel a little better, but it was getting scary sitting on the creek bank as it was getting darker.

"Mr. Gabe, do you want to go across the street and sit on Grandpa's porch?"

"Sure, help me gather up my stuff."

# CHAPTER 7

# Forgiveness

Josh carried the fishing pole, and Gabriel carried his tackle box. They crossed the street and climbed the steps, and Gabe sat on the porch with his feet on the first step. Josh tried to open the door, but it was locked. Josh put down the pole and sat down on the porch. He shivered. When he wrapped the rug that lay on the floor around himself, the fishing pole flipped off the porch down into the bushes. Neither one saw it fall.

Gabriel looked out to the street as a car drove by. "So, what are you going to do now?"

A streetlight cast a little light on the porch;

Josh could only see the silhouette of the old man against the low light. "I don't know. I guess I can sleep here on the porch tonight."

"Will you ever go back to school?"

"I don't know. I can't face those kids making fun of me any more."

Gabe turned to look at Josh and asked, "What are you going to do about Mike?"

"What do you mean?" Josh asked.

"You were really angry with him, and you were fighting with him."

"Yea, but he started it by calling me names."

"True. But what did you gain by fighting with him?"

Josh looked down at the ground. "I don't know; I was just mad."

"Are you going to stay mad at him forever?"

"Probably, forever and ever."

They both watched as another car sped by, and a taxi pulled up to the house three doors down. "Oh, I see. And that will help you feel better?" Gabe asked the boy.

"I don't know, but he deserved it. He's mean for calling me a crybaby. You shouldn't call people names. It hurts."

"Yeah, I would agree with that. It does hurt when people call you names. I wonder if anyone has ever called him a crybaby when he was hurt and cried."

"I don't know." Josh didn't care what happened to Mike.

They both watched as a lady with luggage came out of the house three doors down and stepped into the cab.

Gabe turned to Josh and put his arm around him. "I've always heard that people want to be loved just the way they are. Do you think, just maybe Mike wanted to cry sometimes, but he didn't because he thought no one would love him? Sometimes a person like Mike laughs at others or calls them names when he wants to do what the other person is doing."

"Hmm . . . I never thought about someone loving Mike." They both watched as the cab drove away.

Josh turned to look at Mr. Gabe. "I don't think he'd ever want to cry, though. He's big, and big boys don't cry."

"Yeah, I guess you're right about that. Big boys and men never cry." Gabe turned to look out over the creek again.

Josh continued to look at the side of Gabe's face. "Mr. Gabe, I know men aren't supposed to cry, but my Dad had tears in his eyes at the funeral."

"Hmm, so some men do cry . . . Do you know that the Bible says Jesus cried?"

"Really, Jesus cried?"

"Yes, not once but twice."

"I didn't know that."

"Yes, he cried when his friend Lazarus died and before he entered Jerusalem on Palm Sunday when he was sitting on the donkey up on the hill."

Josh looked over at the creek across the street. *If Jesus cried, maybe I'm not a sissy if I cry.*

The old man gazed at Josh intently. "It seems to me that you have some forgiving to do."

Josh turned his head to look up at Gabe and raised his left eyebrow. "Huh?"

"Maybe you would feel better if you apologized to Mike and forgave him—and yourself."

Josh lowered his head and looked back at his hands. "I don't know . . ."

Gabe gave Josh's shoulder a tender hug. "Forgiving doesn't mean the other person is right and you are wrong. It doesn't mean you will let the person continue to hurt you. Forgiving is letting go of the anger. Letting go of the anger then allows you to look in the eyes of the other person and understand that God and Jesus love him too. Forgiving allows you to heal inside; carrying anger with you just keeps hurting your insides."

Josh sat awhile thinking. "And that's the

inside part that is supposed to become more like Jesus?" he finally asked.

"Yep." Gabe looked back over the creek. "I guess you have some pretty big decisions to make."

# CHAPTER 8

# Dad

Josh began to fidget with the tassels of the rug. "Well, what am I supposed to do? Grandpa's gone, and I don't have anyone to talk to about these things."

"What about your dad?"

"Ah, he's too busy with work. Every time I want to do something with him, he has to work."

"But didn't you and your father go fishing together just recently?"

"Well, we did go fishing once since Grandpa died, but it wasn't the same."

"Why?"

"Because Grandpa wasn't there!"

"Oh." Gabe got up and moved his tackle box over to the side. Sitting down on the porch once again, he stretched out his legs. "Did your dad know how to fish?"

"Yeah, he even knew the secret way to wrap the worm around the hook."

"Well, I wonder who taught him that secret."

Josh sat quiet for a while. "Do you think maybe Grandpa took my dad fishing when he was a little boy? I never thought about that before."

"I wonder what else your dad knows."

"He helps me with my homework—especially arithmetic. He's real smart when it comes to numbers. He also knows a lot about old people and old things."

"What do you mean by old people and old things?"

"You know, back in the old days when there were battles and wars."

"Oh, you mean history."

"Yeah, we once went to Antietam

Battlefield, and Dad told me all about the bloodiest day of the battle. And when we went to the Inner Harbor, Dad told me about how the ships used to come right up into the harbor. We even went to Washington DC one time, but we didn't see the President. We went up all those steps to the top of the Washington Monument, and we saw a statue of Abraham Lincoln sitting in a big chair and the Vietnam wall with all those names written on it."

"It sounds like your dad is a pretty smart guy."

"Yeah, I guess so." Josh shivered a little bit and wrapped the rug tighter around his shoulders. They were quiet for a long time as Gabe leaned back against the wooden post holding up the roof over the porch.

"Mr. Gabe, who will take care of me now?"

"Well, you are nine years old. Maybe you're big enough to take care of yourself."

"I guess so, but I'm still afraid. I brought my bear with me."

"Oh, good. Let's see Oscar."

*Oscar? Gabe even knows the name of my bear!*

Josh rummaged around in his backpack and pulled out Oscar. One of his books tumbled out too.

"Ah, what do we have here?" Gabe said as he put his legs back down on the step and reached for the book.

Josh pulled Oscar under the rug and felt warm and secure. "Would you read to me?"

"I'll have to turn it here so I can see it in the beam from the streetlight."

Gabe began to read the story about the penguins. Josh rolled sideways and lay down on the floor of the porch. He heard the hum of the old man's voice, and his eyelids grew heavier and heavier.

Soon Josh was asleep and began to dream about Grandpa standing on the side of a creek. It looked like the creek where they went fishing, but everything was different. The sun shone brightly and the colors of the trees, the butterflies, and the grass were all dazzling. The creek was bigger and clearer—more like a river—and the birds were chirping happily. Everything seemed full of joy. It seemed that even the fish in the river were smiling.

Grandpa looked up the hill where a bright light was shining; he had a wide smile on his face. A man in blue jeans walked across the water, went up to Grandpa, and held out his hand. Grandpa looked at the man, then looked back over his shoulder, paused, and rubbed his chin with his hand. The man waited. After a few minutes, Grandpa turned back to the man, smiled, let the man help him up, and they crossed the river together. Both men sat down on the other side of the riverbank and began to talk. They nodded their heads, and Grandpa began gesturing with his hands. When the other man lifted his head, Josh saw that he was Jesus.

Then Grandpa stood up and hugged a lady and two men who were walking up to him. Grandpa took the lady's hand, and they all sat down and gathered around Jesus. The bright light from atop the hill was shining on them all, and their faces were radiant—even their clothes were bright and shiny. Then Grandpa pulled out the picture of Josh and the big fish and showed it to everyone.

Jesus took the picture, examined it carefully, and said, "I remember those days!" Then he raised his head and gave a big laugh.

Josh heard Grandpa say, "My grandson, Josh, is a character, but he'll be fine. Josh will be okay."

"JOSH, ARE YOU OKAY? Josh, are you okay?" Josh sleepily opened his eyes to see his dad and mom kneeling beside him. A bright light was shining in his eyes. Josh rubbed his eyes. *Where am I?*

"We've been looking for you for hours. We were here once before. Where have you been?" Mom was hugging him and scolding him at the same time.

"Are you warm? Are you okay? What made

you do such a thing?" His mom was wiping away tears that were sliding down her cheek.

Josh realized he was on Grandpa's porch, and the porch light was on. "I'm sorry, but I knew you would be angry with me once you heard about the fight at school."

"I'm not angry with you. Your teacher called and told me about the fight. She also told me you're having a hard time since your grandfather passed away."

Josh touched his chest. "Yeah, I have this sadness down inside, but Mr. Gabe talked to me and helped me to understand things better."

"Who's Mr. Gabe?" Dad asked as he looked around but saw no one.

Josh pulled away from his mom and looked for the old man.

"He was just here. He looked like Grandpa."

"Josh, there's no one here. No one was here when we showed up, unlocked the door, and turned on the light." Dad looked at Josh and raised his left eyebrow.

Josh rubbed his eyes again and blinked to be sure he was seeing okay.

"He was just sitting there reading to me. Where's my book?" Josh grabbed his backpack and started taking everything out. Both books were there.

"But he was just there." Josh pointed to the place where Gabe had been sitting.

"Come on, let's get you home," Mom said as she began to pick up Oscar and the backpack and to help Josh to his feet.

Dad went in the door to turn off the light when Josh saw the light reflecting off the shiny guide hooks on the fishing rod. "Look, there's Gabe's fishing pole. We were over by the creek fishing earlier. Where's his tackle box?"

"That must be one of Grandpa's old fishing poles, and I don't see a tackle box." Dad picked up the rod and put it inside the door, turned off the light, and locked the door.

Confused, Josh sat in the back seat of the car. He must have dreamed about Gabe. But he did feel better. The heavy sadness was not so heavy any more.

"Josh, are you hungry? Do you want something to eat?" Mom asked.

"No, Mr. Gabe gave me a really good sandwich and an apple," Josh said without thinking. Mom and Dad turned their heads and looked at each other. *If he had only dreamed about the old man, why wasn't he hungry?*

"Dad, can we stop at the cemetery on the way home?"

"I don't know; it's getting late. We need to be getting home."

"Just for a minute, please."

As they drove into the cemetery, the fog began to settle in. Josh walked to his grandfather's grave and looked down at it and up into the dark sky. He couldn't see much for the fog, so he stood for a long time, just wondering.

"I don't understand it all, but I'm not so sad

anymore," Josh mumbled as Mom and Dad watched. "Take care of my grandpa and me, Jesus. Oh, and one more thing. I do want my inside part to become more like you," Josh prayed.

Dad walked up and put his hand on Josh's shoulder. "Grandpa's going to be fine in heaven."

"Yeah, I know. In my dream I saw Grandpa and Jesus laughing."

Dad looked at Josh and smiled. "That's a wonderful thought. I like that. Now, it's time for you to be happy, and you have some pretty big decisions to make so you will be happy."

Josh turned, cocked his head, and raised his left eyebrow. *That's exactly what Mr. Gabe said.*

"Dad, will you help me? Mr. Gabe said I needed to make a decision about apologizing to Mike. Will you help me know what to say to Mike when I see him again?"

"Sure. Sure, Josh, I'll be there when you need me." Dad and Josh turned and walked toward the car.

As Josh approached the car, he looked over his shoulder. In the fog above Grandpa's grave, he saw the face of his grandfather smiling—or was it the face of Mr. Gabe?

# About the Author

An internationally known professor and Reading Specialist who currently teaches at a college which provides learning opportunities to students from over 160 countries, Barbara Jean Van Meter, B.S., M.A., has had many years of experience teaching reading and thinking skills to students who have ranged from pre-school to college level. She also has spent the past ten years teaching a variety of reading strategies to high school teachers for Maryland State Department of Education certification. She has published professional articles and an inspirational article, and she has presented papers on reading at national and international conferences. A trained Stephen Minister and Stephen Leader, she has ministered to those who know grief. She currently resides in Maryland.

You may contact the author through her website at http://sites.google.com/site/barbarajeanvanmeter where you may order books or arrange speaking engagements.

LaVergne, TN USA
24 September 2010
198364LV00002B/1/P